CRAZY PETS

Author: Moira Butterfield

First published in 2016 by Peters Publishing

120 Bromsgrove Street
Birmingham
West Midlands
B5 6RJ

© Peters Publishing

All rights reserved

ISBN: 978-0-9935457-0-2
Dewey number: 636.0887

Commissioned, designed, edited and project managed for Peters Publishing by Dynamo Limited.

Author: Moira Butterfield
Educational consultant: Gill Matthews

Picture credits:

Corbis: Steve Vidler/Corbis p4(b), HO/Reuters/Corbis p8, Louis Quail/In Pictures/Corbis p11(b), Sharpshooter Images/Splash p15(b), Hendrik Schmidt/dpa/Corbis p18(t), Paul Brown/Demotix/Corbis p22, DAN RIEDLHUBER/Reuters/Corbis p28.

Getty: Sean Gallup/Staff p7(b), James L. Stanfield/Contributor p10, Paul Zahi/Contributor p21(t), Barcroft/Contributor 13(t), Colin McConnell/Contributor p13(b), Barcroft/Contributor p29(t), Barcroft/Contributor p29(b).

Shutterstock: Purino p7(t), Volt Collection p9(t), Elias H. Debbas II p12, Jaguar PS p15(t), Neftali p15(m), JStone p14, bluedogroom p25(t). All graphics and vector art from Shutterstock.

iStock: dinoforlena p5(t), photographereddie p5(b), vtis p6, eve_eve01genesis p9(b), GlobalP p11(t), Cynoclub p16(m), Laures p17(t), Evgeny Sergeev p18(b), WilleeCole p19(b), dinoforlena p19(m), Dixi_ p19(t), Gordonimages p20, hansgertbroeder p21(b), jswinborne p23(t), pishit p23(b), segeyryshov p24, HannamariaH p26(t), Mladich p26(b), kuban_girl p27(t), WedSubstance p27(b).

Cover images: Front: Paul Brown/Demotix/Corbis (tl), Mladich (tr), HO/Reuters/Corbis (bl), JStone (br). Back: pishit (tr), bluedogroom (mr), Paul Zahi/Contributor (bl).

Every attempt has been made to clear copyright. Should there be any inadvertent omission, please apply to the publisher for rectification.

Printed in the United Kingdom

Peters Publishing is an imprint of Peters Books and Furniture
120 Bromsgrove Street
Birmingham
West Midlands
B5 6RJ

www.peters-books.co.uk

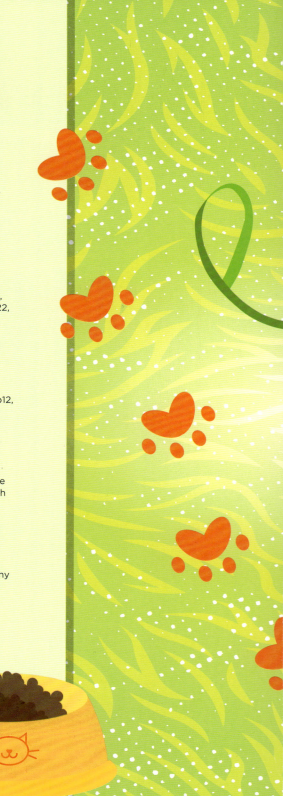

CONTENTS

- 4 Pets Long Ago
- 6 Big Pets
- 8 Tiny Pets
- 10 Clever Pets
- 12 Brave Pets
- 14 Celebrity Pets
- 16 Crazy-looking Dogs
- 18 Crazy-looking Cats
- 20 Watery Wonders
- 22 Creepy-crawlies
- 24 Reptile Pets
- 26 Pet Presents
- 28 Craziest Pets Ever
- 30 Quiz
- 31 Glossary
- 32 Answers

PETS LONG AGO

People have been mad about pets for thousands of years! Here are some crazy pet facts from history.

CAT IN A WRAP

The Ancient Egyptians turned their pet cats into mummies when they died.

They believed the dead cats went to live in another world, and would still need their bodies.

Cat mummies like this one had a cat face drawn on the front.

Roman pet eels wore tiny necklaces, and earrings on their fins.

HEEL, EEL!

The Ancient Romans kept eels as pets. The eels were trained to swim over when their names were called.

POSH NOSH

The pets of Roman Emperors had the very best treatment. Emperor Caligula gave his favourite horse gold flakes in its food.

BIG PETS

These furry friends tip the scales as record-breaking big pets.

WHAT A DOG!

Great Danes are the world's biggest dogs. They can grow over a metre tall. Luckily, they are gentle and friendly.

Great Danes can grow as long as a sofa!

MONSTER RODENT

The capybara looks like an enormous guinea pig. Here's what you need to know.

- They grow as big as a medium-sized dog.
- They love salad.
- They purr.

HEFTY HOPPER

The biggest pet rabbit of all is the German Giant. This massive bunny is very cuddly, but very expensive too. It can cost around £50 a week to feed.

The German Giant can grow two times as long as a cat.

TINY PETS

These mini pets are crazy but cute. Everybody say "Ah!".

SMALL BUT PERFECT

The world's tiniest horse is called Einstein. He is around 35 centimetres tall. That's the size of a small dog. He is a breed of horse called a Falabella.

Einstein the horse plays with a much bigger friend, Hannah the dog.

SMALL SCALE

Mini goats are much smaller than normal goats. They are very clever and can learn to walk on a lead, like a dog.

Mini goats don't like to be on their own. They need friends!

PRICKLY PET

African mini hedgehogs live in a cage like hamsters. But unlike hamsters, they eat meat. They enjoy cat food and live insects, too. Yum!

CLEVER PETS

Pets have got talent! Some of them can learn clever skills.

PET TRAINING

Pet rats are very clever. They can fetch balls and jump through hoops. They can learn their name and come when you call. Some will even shake paws with you.

This boy has taught his rat to walk on a tightrope.

BRAINY BIRD

Parrots can learn to say words and do tricks, such as riding tiny bikes. They like to play too, so it's a good idea to buy them toys.

PET WINNERS

Dog dancing competitions are popular at dog shows. Dog owners dance with their pets and show off clever tricks to win. The owner might get their dog to roll over or jump as part of the dance.

An exciting dog dance move.

BRAVE PETS

Here are some furry friends who have made amazing rescues or shown great bravery.

HISTORY HERO

Balto was a brave American dog. He battled through snow and ice for six days to carry medicine to a town in Alaska. Balto now has his own statue in New York.

The statue of brave Balto in New York, USA.

LEARNING TO WALK

Corky the cat was born with his back legs the wrong way round. Thanks to an operation, he can now take steps. Every day Corky has training to help him learn to walk again.

Corky the cat works hard to walk.

BEARS DON'T SCARE ME!

Jarod the dog saved his owner's life. He fought off a black bear when it attacked her.

Jarod the dog won a medal for his bravery.

CELEBRITY PETS

Some pets are superstars, with lots of fans around the world.

MOVIE STARS

Lassie was probably the most famous movie star dog ever. Lassie movies and TV shows were shown all over the world for many years.

CROSS KITTY

Grumpy Cat is an internet star because of her online videos. Now her funny face is on t-shirts, mugs and books. She has earned her owner a lot of money. Meow!

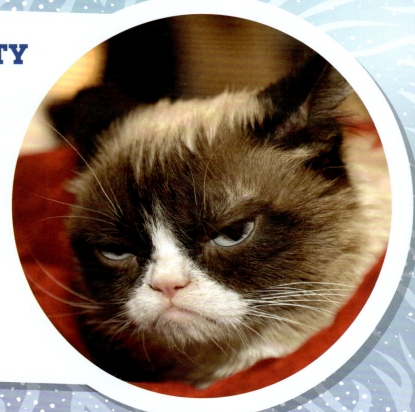

Uggie was a little dog with big fame. He appeared in several smash hit movies and won top awards for his roles.

Uggie at the Academy Awards in Hollywood.

Lassie was so famous she was put on a stamp.

INTERNET STARS

Singer Taylor Swift's pet cats star in their own online videos. They even have Twitter accounts.

CRAZY-LOOKING DOGS

Dogs come in all shapes and sizes. Here are three of the funniest doggie pets you'll find.

CRAZY BUT CUTE!

Chinese Crested Hairless dogs look very strange. Their body is almost bald, but their head is very hairy. They're not pretty, but they're fun!

Chinese Crested Hairless dogs often win prizes for ugliness.

HAPPY CHAP?

This dog could beat Grumpy Cat for the funniest frown. It has a better beard, too! It is a kind of dog called a Brussels Griffon.

Cheer up, grumpy dog!

MAD MOP

The Puli dog has so much thick hair that it looks like a cuddly floor mop. Puli dogs can be black or white, but they always look cute.

The Puli dog's coat of tight curls is almost waterproof.

CRAZY-LOOKING CATS

These purring pussy cats stand out for their unusual looks.

AMAZING EARS

The American Curl cat gets its name from its ears, which curl back. They look more like bats' ears than cats' ears!

COLD CAT

The Ukrainian Levkoy cat is almost bald, so it can't go outside in cold weather. Poor kitty!

SILKY SOFT

The Cornish Rex cat has huge ears and a silky-soft, curly coat.

MINI KITTY

The Munchkin cat has very short legs, but it loves to jump and run around.

Is that a weird-looking rabbit? No. It's a Cornish Rex cat.

WATERY WONDERS

You don't need to take underwater pets for a walk. You can just watch them swimming round and round and round and round. You get the idea!

WHAT A SUCKER!

This funny-looking fish is called a pleco. Its mouth looks like a big sucker. It sucks up tiny plants called algae (al-gee), helping to keep its tank clean.

The pleco always eats with its mouth open! It sucks its food in.

FUNNY FISH

Goldfish come in lots of different shapes and sizes. Some unusual ones have strange bumps and bulges on their faces. Others have bubble-shaped eyes.

Bubble-eye goldfish have their eyes on top of their head.

MERRY CHRISTMAS!

You can have a Christmas tree as a pet! It is a type of water worm that can be kept in an aquarium. It looks like a little tree growing on a piece of rock.

CREEPY-CRAWLIES

These pets are not exactly cuddly. They creep and crawl — but some people think they're cute!

FRUIT FAN!

Giant African snails like to eat cucumber, apple and banana. A snail is not a 'he' or a 'she'. It is both male and female, so you could give it any name you like!

This Giant African snail is called Shelley. It's a boy and a girl in one.

THAT'S BIG!

The Giant African millipede is a gentle pet. It doesn't mind being picked up, and likes to munch on fruit and vegetables. It can grow up to 400 legs.

A Giant African millipede can grow up to 25 centimetres long.

INSECT FRIENDS

Rhino (rye-no) beetles are a popular pet in Japan. The Goliath (gol-eye-ath) beetle is the biggest and heaviest one. It can grow up to 15 centimetres long.

Japanese shops sell banana flavoured jelly for pet beetles to eat.

REPTILE PETS

Snakes and lizards make unusual pets, but they are hard to look after. They are only for true reptile fans.

ARE YOU SURE?

Really big snakes need very careful owners. Here are three facts that might put you off owning one.

- Really big snakes can squeeze people to death.
- Some pet snakes will only eat live animals.
- Pet snakes can live for up to 30 years.

RARE REPTILE

The albino ball python has a rare and lovely skin pattern. It is one of the most expensive pets in the world.

An albino ball python can cost up to £9,600.

£9,600

ROOM HOG

Iguanas are sometimes kept as pets, but they need a lot of space. They eat vegetables and fruit and can grow as long as a sofa!

PET PRESENTS

Owners can spend millions on jewellery, designer outfits and holidays for their pets. Is that crazy? You decide!

BLING! BLING!

Owners can buy diamond collars and tiaras for their pets, along with gold food bowls. There is even a luxury doggie perfume — and for cats there's a diamond-covered cat flap!

Spot the sparkle. This dog is wearing a diamond tiara.

PET FASHION

There are all sorts of outfits for pets — especially cats and dogs. Owners sometimes even give their pets weddings, and dress them in up wedding outfits.

PERFECT FOR PETS

Pet hotels offer luxury holidays for pets. They have the very best pet beds, food and flat screen TVs — and even swimming pools!

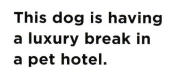

This dog is having a luxury break in a pet hotel.

CRAZIEST PETS EVER

Here are some pets that you won't see every day. Imagine owning one of these!

GOING LARGE

This buffalo is called Bailey Junior, and he lives in Canada. He likes to go inside his owners' home. They looked after him when he was a baby, so he is very tame.

Bailey the buffalo pops into the kitchen.

GIVE ME A KISS!

This crocodile, called Pocho, was a very famous pet in Costa Rica. His owner Chito often performed with him. When Pocho died he had a big funeral because he was so famous.

Einstein the skunk goes for a walk with his owner Hannah.

MINI MARVELS

This little pet skunk, called Einstein, goes everywhere with his owner. He has had an operation so that he doesn't spray stinky smells like wild skunks.

QUIZ

How much do you know about crazy pets? Test yourself with this quiz! The answers are on page 32.

1. Who made their pet cats into mummies?

a) The Romans
b) The Ancient Egyptians
c) The Ancient Greeks

2. What is a Great Dane?

a) A dog
b) A cat
c) A rabbit

3. What is a Falabella?

a) A horse
b) A goat
c) A sheep

4. What does a Puli dog look like?

a) A cat
b) A floor mop
c) A small horse

5. Why can't Levkoy cats go outside in cold weather?

6. In Japan some people keep a type of insect as a pet. Which type of insect?

a) The fighting ant
b) The rhino beetle
c) The boxing beetle

7. Is this true or false?

Some large snakes can squeeze other animals to death.

GLOSSARY

Academy Awards — important movie awards, also called the Oscars.

algae — tiny plant-like growths. Algae often grow in water.

Ancient Egyptians — people who lived in Egypt around 5,000 years ago.

breed — a particular type of animal. A poodle is a breed of dog, for example.

capybara — a type of animal that looks like a giant guinea pig.

Falabella — a type of tiny horse.

pleco — a type of fish.

reptile — an animal from the group of creatures that includes snakes, lizards and iguanas.

scale — the size of something. Scale can also mean the tiny plates on the skins of fish or snakes.

ANSWERS

1. The Ancient Egyptians made their pet cats into mummies.

2. A Great Dane is a type of dog.

3. A Falabella is a type of horse.

4. A Puli dog looks like a floor mop.

5. Levkoy cats are almost bald, so they cannot keep themselves warm outside in cold weather.

6. Rhino beetles are sometimes kept as pets in Japan.

7. It is true. Some large snakes can squeeze other animals to death.